But God, Wouldn't I Be More Useful to You If I Were Healthy?

Chronic Pain and the Christian Life Series

ESTHER SMITH

But God, Wouldn't I Be More Useful to You
If I Were Healthy?

Visit the author's website at lifeinslowmotionblog.com.

Contents

CHAPTER 1

Called but Physically Unable

I remember the night all too clearly, yet pieces of it are a blur. The night was awash with emotions. I was spending a college semester in Uganda, studying abroad at a university among a small group of Americans and local Ugandans. Our American group had just returned from our homestays, each of us living for a week with different families in the rural Soroti District.

Envision pictures you've seen in National Geographic. Think of small huts in the middle of the African bush. Seven days of eating with my hands and sitting on the ground. Seven days of shelling ground nuts with the children, making dinner over the fire, and sweeping out the compound with sticks. Seven days of waking up at dawn, fetching water, and sponge bathing under the open starry sky.

This experience gave me more than enough time to think about life and what it's really about. Time to consider the purposelessness of materialism, the selfishness that perpetuates society, and the ideals of real community. There was something calming about the stillness and peace of rural village life. I remember the soothing feeling of sitting and shelling ground nuts all day in relative quiet, and then lying down for an afternoon nap while the hot sun baked the compound. The work was difficult, but life was simple, and much good came out of that simplicity.

The night we all came back and reunited after our individual homestays was chaotic. So many returned with stories and unforgettable experiences. For many it had been the most difficult and trying week of the semester. For me it had felt so right, so eye-opening, so transformative.

I began frantically journaling in the solitude of my little dorm. In Soroti, I saw a way of living and serving that inspired me. My

4

host mother was a remarkable woman who served in the midst of normal life in simple yet phenomenal ways. I heard her get up at 3 or 4 in the morning to sing and pray until the rest of the family woke at dawn. I watched her give money to any neighbor who asked, though she herself was poor. She raised her children and several orphans with no husband to help or support her.

Day after day she worked hard, prayed hard, loved hard. She was an extraordinary woman who did simple things in big ways, serving with great humility and few resources.

Sitting in my dorm, I scribbled across the pages of my journal. I don't remember the exact words, but I know that I told God, *"Send me. Choose me."* As a college student, I was struck with an awareness that life is about more than finding the perfect job. Life is about more than going on crazy adventures. It has a lot to do with God, and not much to do with me. It has a lot to do with people and generosity and giving of myself, and my concept and definition of those things had just been broadened in a significant way.

I wrote on and on, recalling the simple and tangible acts of service I had observed. I told God, *"Send me anywhere you want, to do anything you want. It doesn't have to be on a crazy adventure. Just your will be done."* I knew I was making a dangerous request. I knew, but I didn't know.

I remember thinking that, perhaps, God would send me to the unexpected. Maybe he would call me to be a good wife, friend, and servant to those around me, and that would be all, but it would be enough, just as it was enough for my host mom. Maybe I wouldn't go on adventures or serve through missions or work in outdoor ministry as I had once imagined. Perhaps, my ministry would be in the mundane, in the simple, in the everyday.

When Chronic Pain Enters Our Lives

Looking back and recalling that night, I realize that I could not have been more right and more wrong at the same time. A year after I returned from my semester abroad, chronic pain entered my life. Chronic pain took hold, and I crossed the border of health into a parallel universe of sickness. I walked into a cross-cultural world of pain and suffering that exists right next to those in good health, but follows a completely different set of customs, rules, and expectations.

Even now, as I look back on my worst months and years of chronic pain with the help of space and growth, I feel incapable of describing the physical and emotional intensity of severe chronic pain in a way that does not feel like exaggerating. I feel unable to describe the seconds that felt like hours, the flares that left me unable to leave the house for days, and the weeks when I could do nothing but lie there and pray that God would get me through.

How do I describe the way pain ripped through my body and my soul? How do I describe looking normal, pretending to be normal, but feeling like I might collapse? How do I describe the way it never, not for a moment, not for a second, ended or relented?

I recently looked back through my journals, and memories of that night flooded my mind and jolted my stomach. Is this what I was saying yes to? Was I saying yes to years of sickness and pain? I told God, *"Please send me where I can serve you best. My life is open, completely set aside for you."* Was chronic pain what I asked for?

Just as I imagined that night, God sent me to the last place I ever could have expected. And just like I wondered, it was a place that was ordinary, mundane, and certainly not glamorous in any way. But he didn't just call me to the mundane. He called me to the painful mundane, the suffering mundane, the limited mundane. This was not the mundane of motherhood – the endless diapers, meals, and midnight comforts. This was the mundane of nothingness – the inability to do much of anything. This was not the mundane of the 9-5 – the endless meetings, number crunching, and dealing with difficult people. This was the mundane of isolation – the endless naps, distractions, and days with little contact with the outside world.

Life felt exceedingly purposeless, and no amount of spinning it around in my head could convince me that lying on the couch in pain was part of building up the Kingdom of God. Nothing could convince me that chronic pain had anything to do with service or my desire to do God's work. For many years, life was filled with uncertainty, and I struggled to determine why God would force me to while my time away in pain, unused, unneeded, and perhaps even unwanted.

When Work and Service Feel Impossible

In my pre-pain body, I never could have imagined how confusing it would be to live out a biblical call to work, while still maintaining the rest that is needed to care for a chronic pain condition.

Truthfully, chronic pain is exhausting. Life-sucking, hit-by-a-truck, unable-to-get-out-of-bed exhausting. The exhaustion of chronic pain is unlike the normal tiredness faced by healthy people with busy lives. The tiredness we face never goes away no matter how much we sleep or how much we rest. We are so tired and in so much pain, but we live in a busy world that expects people to go, go, go, and the question of "How much should I do?" is on constant play in our minds. Most of us do not have this aspect of chronic pain figured out, as evidenced by the surprising amount of guilt that plagues us when we are forced to stop. We feel guilty that we are no longer able to work like we used to, forcing others to take up our slack. Not only are others carrying our load of work, but at times they are also burdened with being our caretakers, helping us manage our conditions to various degrees.

Setbacks, relapses, and huge flares that last for weeks, months, or even years on end can result when those in chronic pain do not carefully monitor the amount of work, service, and active movement done in a given day or time period. At times, extra pain is a worthwhile cost for extra movement, but other times we look back in regret on activities we completed that led to serious health consequences, desiring to take back the decision to push ourselves too far.

We feel caught between a rock and a hard place. Too much work leads to flares and relapse; too much rest leads to feelings of guilt and worthlessness. We try to walk the middle, but this feels like an impossible balancing act on a razor-thin tightrope.

Since pain became a constant part of my life, no question has plagued me more than the question of work and service. No commands have irked me more than God's commands to do good works (Titus 3:14), serve (I Peter 4:10), and love others in tangible ways. God wrote these verses in clear and direct ways, but with chronic pain, they don't seem so clear anymore. How do we practically obey these Scriptures when physically doing things is difficult, dangerous, or even impossible?

Chronic pain forces me – and many others like me – to live through long periods of time when I only have enough energy to care for myself. Instead of loving my neighbors or going to work, I am stuck lying down, feeling unproductive and alone. At times, feelings of embarrassment form as I begin to wonder what others think about me. What do my friends think when I always say no? What do people at church think when I am always absent and never participate in service opportunities? What do people at work think when I do the bare minimum required of me? *Why is this happening to me?*

I have had many long and teary conversations with God about this topic, conversations filled with questions, confusion, anger, and doubt. At times I have felt angry at God for giving me a heart to serve and a body that just couldn't. *"God that is confusing!"* When I read verses that depict service as an expected and natural aspect of the Christian life, sometimes I want to throw my Bible across the room. *"God, that just feels mean to tell me all Christians serve, but then leave me whiling my time away in bed."* An inability to enact the life I once envisioned has been demoralizing and weary to my soul. *"God, are you sure you are not making a mistake?"*

That night in Soroti, I told God I was willing to do anything, to serve him in any way, but I never, not once, considered the possibility that he would make service impossible for me. I never considered how I would respond if God took all of my good plans and threw them in the trash, telling me he had something else in store for me.

"God," I say, *"Why would you keep me from serving? Why would you choose me of all people? Me who wants to serve and work and would dedicate my life to you if you would just let me. Aren't I good at serving? Don't I make a difference?* The desire to do more wells up inside, sadness and guilt rising to the surface. And I am ashamed to remember times when I have said to God, *"Why Lord? Think of all the things I could do for you, if I weren't so physically limited?*

Chapter 1 Journaling Questions

1. What is your story of work in the midst of chronic pain or illness? What have you lost when it comes to your career, ministry, or ability to serve?

2. What questions do you have for God when it comes to this topic of working and serving with chronic pain or illness?

CHAPTER 2

Sitting at the Feet of Jesus

More times than I can count, prayers of pride and doubt have reverberated through my mind. *But God, wouldn't I be more useful to you if I were healthy?* And I realize now that underneath my words I have bargained with God. I have told God that I would work for him if he healed me. I would do great things for his Kingdom if he would realize his mistake and make things right.

Many times I have become blinded and failed to recognize the pride that underlies what I once saw as a humble desire to serve the Lord. One of the reasons I miss my ability to work is because work gives me something to boast in, something to point to that shows how "great" I am and how "needed" I am for progress to happen. *Work gives me status and worth in society, and when I have to stop, I am forced to look at who I am without the work that once made me feel needed.*

Is anyone else with me? Does anyone else need God to step on these delusions and show us a different and better way? God's promises concerning work pull us away from prideful motivations. His promises rescue us from our feelings of guilt for being a "nobody" in a world that prizes work and accomplishments above all else. God promises us that work is not the most important part of the Christian life.

The gospel doesn't begin with a call to work, but with a call to believe and a gift we receive. We rest in the promise of Ephesians 2:8-9 which tells us, "For by grace you have been saved through faith. And this is not your own doing; it is the gift of God, not a result of works, so that no one may boast." The salvation of God, Christ's death on the cross to blot out our sins and grant us hope of a future with him, is a gift that no amount of work can earn. We begin by resting in the salvation God freely gives.

Because chronic pain takes away so much of our ability to work and to do, we have been freed from our ability to boast. *Chronic pain forces us to wrestle with the underlying thought, deep down inside of us all, that maybe we are worth more when we do more.* We are forced to face the lie we hate to admit we believe, this blatant, dangerous lie so antithetical to the gospel God gives, that the greater our works the greater our worth.

God's truth opposes this lie. The truth is that because of what Christ has done, we are free to simply be. Work makes us no more valuable, loved, precious, treasured, important, or saved in the eyes of God. Doing more does not make us worth more. When chronic pain takes away our ability to do and to work, we do not become worth less. Because of what Christ has done, we are free to exist in his presence, held up by his grace, and that is enough.

Only One Thing Is Needed

All my life I was a Martha until pain stopped me in my tracks. Do you know the story? Martha is a woman in Scripture who opens up her home to Jesus and his disciples. Always the good hostess, Martha bustles around with preparations, making sure everything is just right. She looks and sees that her sister, Mary, isn't helping her with any of the work. No, Mary is sitting at Jesus' feet and listening to him.

Martha becomes upset. She asks Jesus to tell Mary to get up and start helping. Jesus' response to Martha is so wonderful. His response is so beautiful and so right, as Jesus' responses always are. "'Martha, Martha,' the Lord answered, 'you are worried and upset about many things, but few things are needed – or indeed only one. Mary has chosen what is better, and it will not be taken away from her'" (Luke 10:41,42).

I am too much like Martha for comfort. Getting up to serve makes me feel better about myself and like I am contributing. I feel more comfortable with work than with sitting at the feet of Jesus. Sitting and doing nothing is so uncomfortable. There are things to do, places to go, and work to be done. What good comes out of sitting and wasting time away?

I would still be scurrying around and forgetting about Jesus because of my oh-so-important work if it weren't for chronic pain. Through the limitations of chronic pain, Jesus has invited me to stop, pause, and listen. He invites all of us to rest in him, worship him, and remain still before him as he speaks to us.

This is the one thing that is needed. *This* is the choice that Jesus called "better." *This* is the thing that cannot be taken away. Like Martha, we have grounded ourselves in work that is a fleeting and passing thing of this world; it is no wonder we feel confused, depressed, and guilty when chronic pain stops us in our tracks and keeps us from doing what used to give us meaning.

Resting at the Feet of Jesus

Just as he said to the apostles, Jesus says to you and to me, "Come with me by yourselves to a quiet place and get some rest" (Mark 6:31). Most of us with chronic pain give everything that we have on a daily basis, every last drop of our limited supply of energy and physical strength to get through each day. And then we feel guilty that we do not have more to give like everyone else. Like the apostles we are weary and tired, burdened and burned out. Will we accept Jesus' invitation to rest at his feet?

It can be difficult to accept this invitation. Many days, I look at all that is being accomplished around me and feel guilty for needing and wanting to rest. The thought of one more day spent lying on the couch feels like torture. But I believe Jesus sees it in a different way. Rest in the physical sense is not a thing of guilt; rest is a thing of faith. It requires faith to walk away from our work and ministry when progress is being made. It requires faith to put a halt to all the things we were accomplishing in our healthier state. It requires faith to walk with Jesus away from our burdens and work, resting our bodies and souls in him.

Let me give you a practical picture of what I believe faithful rest looks like in a life of chronic pain. It sounds and feels counterintuitive, but I believe that sometimes the most faithful thing we can possibly do is *not work.*

When all I want to do is join the world in a guilt-driven flurry of activities that I am unable to keep up with, the simple act of taking a nap becomes an extravagant expression of faith. In faith, I sleep when all I want is to do. In faith, I leave my kitchen dirty, knowing my worth has no connection to sparkling countertops. In faith, I quit going to Bible Study, stopped serving in children's ministry, and quit a job that allowed me to help many in need. Wait, I stopped doing these things *in faith*? Yes, I believe these were acts of faith. I knew these activities were bringing about uncontrollable flaring and relapse. So in faith, I chose not to prove what I could do to the point of permanent harm; I chose to rest.

I am learning to have faith that my work is before God and not before men, and at times I say "no" to adding things to my schedule even when others do not understand. God sees and knows the heart of man. He sees when my "no" is an act of faith and not an act of defiance or complacency. He sees when my heart is saying "I don't have to prove myself to the detriment of my health. I don't have to say 'yes' to be valuable, worthy, or saved. Only God can give me value, worth, and salvation."

In faith, I allow others to see me rest, and I am learning to feel no guilt. I am learning to invite others into my home where they can see my un-mopped floors and empty calendar. I am learning that I have nothing to hide. I am learning to invite people over when I am sprawled on the floor or couch, covered in heating pads and ice packs and sipping my tea. In faith, I am learning to rest in the presence of others, free from guilt, pretense, and shame.

A true understanding of Scripture finds that serving is not optional, but neither is rest. Rest is an expression of faith, trust, and obedience. Rest puts us in our rightful place, reminding us that it is God, and not us, who is at work, managing the tide and course of all that befalls this world.

Worshiping at the Feet of Jesus

The most precious part of rest is that it frees us up to fulfill our primary purpose, the reason God created us in the first place. Many of us have become confused, believing that God created us first and foremost to work, but he had something far greater, far more glorious in mind.

What is the chief end of man? Perhaps you have memorized this question in the Westminster Catechism. I know that I did as a child, but why is it so hard to recall and actually apply to my life? The answer reads, "Man's chief end is to glorify God, and to enjoy him forever."1 When God created us, he made us for a specific reason: "Thou art worthy, O Lord, to receive glory and honour and power: for thou hast created all things, and for thy pleasure they are and were created" (Revelations 4:11, KJV). We were created for God's pleasure, and what brings him pleasure is that we worship him, praise him, and adore him forever.

My friend Nancy embodies what it means to sit at Jesus' feet as Mary did, listening to him, learning from him, and worshipping him. Listen to her story.

Nancy was born with primary erythromelalgia, a rare pain condition she inherited from her mother. This condition affects all four of her limbs, and Nancy says that when warm temperatures trigger an erythromelalgia flare, the pain feels like someone is pouring boiling water over her body. For many years, even as she dealt with constant pain, Nancy was able to work as a beauty therapist, a job she loved for the contact it provided her with other people. In 1997 she opened up a beauty salon in her home, allowing her to work as she raised her children.

In 2004, an ankle injury would lead to the diagnosis of yet another devastating pain condition. While walking on uneven ground at a picnic, Nancy tore a ligament in her right ankle. In 2005, she had necessary ankle reconstruction surgery, but when the caste was taken off several weeks later, the surgeon diagnosed her with complex regional pain syndrome (CRPS) in her leg.

CRPS is a pain condition that can be triggered by physical trauma or surgery. In Nancy's case, the CRPS was triggered by the surgeon's scalpel as he cut through nerves to reach the damaged ligament. CRPS has been classified as one of the most painful conditions in the world, leaving individuals with constant, 24/7 pain of an intensity higher than childbirth. After several months, the CRPS traveled from Nancy's right leg to her left as well, leaving her with searing, burning, electrifying pain from the knees down.

Even after the diagnosis of CRPS, Nancy was able to work for about two hours each day as a beauty therapist. During this time, Nancy found some relief through a combination of pain medications, physical therapy, counseling, and hydrotherapy. For ten years she attended hydrotherapy four to five times a week, as it gave her just enough relief to make it through the next twenty-four hours. Though the pain was constant and severe, Nancy was still able to do small amounts of cooking and cleaning. She was still able to drive for up to thirty minutes in the car, maintaining some of her independence.

In 2014, disaster struck. At one of her hydrotherapy sessions, an accident took place in the pool. A heavy-set man in his seventies attempted to hoist himself out of the pool instead of safely walking up the pool ramp. As he tried to lift himself over the edge, he slipped and grabbed the person closest to him to break his fall. That person was Nancy. Although the man sustained no injury, the consequences for Nancy were devastating. The impact of this accident caused the CRPS to spread throughout her entire body leaving her with full-body CRPS. To this day, not one inch of her body remains untouched by the pain.

Since the accident, life has become much smaller for Nancy. Because of the pain, Nancy is no longer able to work as a beauty therapist or in any other formal capacity. She is mostly homebound and only able to leave her house for occasional trips to church and for short errands. The pain that comes from her CRPS has been deemed intractable, which means her doctors believe she has no more treatment options to pursue. Although her church family has stepped in and helped her in numerous ways, she is often isolated and without human contact. Even seeking support online causes Nancy much additional pain due to the movement required to type and scroll on her iPad.

Nancy will live with severe pain for the rest of her life. She will never be able to work as a beauty therapist again, a job she loved that enabled her to serve many people. Losing a career and living much of life in isolation is devastating for all who walk that path. I am sure Nancy would agree that she has many difficult days. But in the midst of difficult days, I am amazed at how Nancy has prioritized worship and communing with God in her life, making this the most important thing. How easy it would be for her to remain bitter at God and maintain a deep anger towards the man who hurt her. But when I hear Nancy speak, her voice is filled with nothing but peace. I believe this is because Nancy lives her life worshipping at the feet of Jesus. Listen to Nancy describe her life with chronic pain.

"We live in a world that is so hurried that when we are forced to rest or receive treatment on an ongoing basis it doesn't feel as if

we are doing much at all. But, if we stop and focus on the many blessings instead of our losses, we become grateful for the time we have to spend in prayer, Bible study and in the presence of God. Very few people will see it that way until the Lord opens their eyes.

I am choosing to view this period of my life as a gift from God. To spend the time wisely reading his Word, studying, memorizing Scripture and applying it to my life. Also spending more time in prayer for others and myself. One of my prayers is that the Lord would make me an instrument of God's love to another hurting individual.

Clearly the Spirit of God is upon Nancy, residing in her heart, granting her a peace that surpasses all understanding. As I listen to Nancy, I am left with so many questions for you and for me when our hearts are filled with a burning desire for a life different than the one we have been given.

What will we do with the time, space, and stillness that God has given us? How will we use our hours of isolation and the long days that feel so empty and devoid of purpose? Can we choose to use this time devoid of work and activity to sit at Jesus' feet and worship him?

Finding Our Identity at the Feet of Jesus

Before chronic pain, I placed so much of myself in my jobs and places of active service. Like Martha, I did good and sincere work for the Lord, but the allegiances of my heart were disordered. I never considered how tightly my worth was tied to doing my job well. I never considered how closely I had connected my identity to my ability to actively serve. When my past avenues and approaches to work were taken from me, I began to wonder who I really was underneath the surface. I didn't have peace like Nancy. I didn't realize, as Nancy has realized, that God might desire me to pursue him instead of a new job. I had so many questions. *Who am I when I cannot work? Where does my meaning come from? Where do I find purpose in life?*

Perhaps God is using chronic pain to wake us up. He is

16

awakening people like you and like me who once defined ourselves by our ability to contribute.

Can you see yourself at your core? Can you see who you are when the mask of work and activity that once defined you is taken away? Christ invites us to find our true identity, *who we are,* in him. Not in the jobs we have lost. Not in the things we cannot do. Not in the people we cannot help or the opportunities we must decline. Not in our inadequacies or limitations; not in our abilities or strengths. Only in who he created us to be – worshipers of the one true God. We are made in his image, purposefully created to glorify him forever and bring him pleasure. *This* is who we are – his children, his people, created by him and for him.

How important it is to never place our purpose, our worth, or our identity in something that can be taken away. When we sit at the feet of Jesus and look to his face, we find something that we will never lose, no matter how bad the pain becomes, no matter how severe our limitations. Rest in his grace when you are unable to work. Sit at the feet of Jesus, for he has called this the one thing that is needed.

Chapter 2 Journaling Questions

1. How are you using your times forced times of rest to worship God, glorify God, and sit at the feet of Jesus? Provide a list of ways this is happening in your life.

2. How would you like to grow in this area? Give some specific examples.

CHAPTER 3

Serving Out of a Poverty of Health

We are free to rest and called to sit at the feet of Jesus, and in the end, it is these acts of love and worship towards God that bring about a desire to work for God. Our callings as workers and worshipers are deeply intertwined. In the book of Romans, Paul says, "Therefore, I urge you, brothers and sisters, in view of God's mercy, to offer your bodies as a living sacrifice, holy and pleasing to God – this is your true and proper worship" (Romans 12:1).

In our worship of him, God asks that we give him all of ourselves. He not only wants our hearts and identities to align with him and his ways, but he asks that our bodies be used as living sacrifices to carry out his work. I don't know about you, but this verse makes me feel inadequate, once again. *God, what use could you ever have for my broken, bruised, and limited body?* I don't feel fit to be a living sacrifice. I don't feel enough. I don't feel able.

A distinct memory is ingrained in my mind of one of my worst seasons of pain. I remember that it was a November, and my husband was going through an important time at work. He was completing a difficult and intense several weeks of training that would hopefully lead to a promotion. I was in one of the worst pain flare ups of my life, and each day was a struggle to survive. Each day I barely managed to handle my own daily tasks of living. Each day I struggled to eat three meals a day, get dressed, and move from my bed to the couch.

I remember considering how I could support my husband through his training, and the only thing I felt physically capable of doing was to make him lunch every day so he would have one less thing to worry about. Every day I made three peanut butter and jelly sandwiches. My life was reduced to bare minimum mode, plus this one extra task each day. Making these sandwiches took me multiple times getting off the couch with rests in-between to get it done. I would get up and take everything out of the fridge. Rest. Put the peanut butter on. Rest. Jelly. Rest. Sandwiches into sandwich bags. Rest. Put everything away. Long rest.

I share this story not because it fills me with pride to remember how I served the best I could in the worst of times, and definitely not because I like people to know how rock bottom I have reached. I share this story because I think back on this time feeling shame, inadequacy, and failure. I think back and see my inability, my lack, and how fully the pain controlled my body. I share this story because I wonder if you feel this way, too, as you serve in small ways, feeling like it is nothing.

How easy it is for shame and feelings of failure to arise when we look around and see others giving so much, while our acts of giving are so small. Our gifts pale in comparison to others who aren't shackled to a body that refuses to move as it should. We begin to wonder if we should leave the serving to the more able-bodied, those individuals who are actually able to make a difference.

Jesus speaks encouraging words to us when our acts of service feel insignificant and unneeded. In the gospel of Luke, we find the story of the widow's mite.

> "As Jesus looked up, he saw the rich putting their gifts into the temple treasury. He also saw a poor widow put in two very small copper coins. 'Truly I tell you,' he said, 'this poor widow has put in more than all the others. All these people gave their gifts out of their wealth; but she out of her poverty put in all she had to live on'" (Luke 21:1-4).

Jesus looked at the widow's small offering and saw anything but insignificance. He was greatly pleased with her sacrifice, despite the small quantity she had to give. Contrary to the ways of this world, Jesus sees service as an act of sacrifice, not a competition to see who can give the most. Just as the widow gave out of a poverty of financial ruin, in the same way, those who live with debilitating chronic pain give out of a poverty of health.

I look back on my small act of making peanut butter and jelly sandwiches and see failure, but I believe Jesus sees something different. I don't believe he sees inadequacy and weakness. I don't think he looks at me and wonder why I did so little. I believe he looks on me and sees sacrifice. I believe he looks and sees me not as inadequate, but as enough, not because of any great thing I have done, but because in my weakness, he is strong. And I believe he looks on you in the same way.

It is likely that no one sees the depths of your courage when you drag yourself out of bed, standing until your bones ache and your muscles burn just to make dinner for your family. No one cheers you on when you painfully drive your children to school each day, just like every parent is expected to do. No one notices that going to work five days a week is a herculean task for you; it is simply expected that you will care for your family.

God notices when you serve in these ways, and he is pleased. He knows that you are giving out of a poverty of health, and he is honored and glorified by your sacrifice. Though your everyday acts of service may seem normal and regular to those around you, God sees that you are giving all that you own.

When unloading the dishwasher is the Mt. Everest you climb every day. When you play with your kids even though it hurts. When your daily commute is the daily cross you bear. When the only chore you can manage is refilling the toilet paper roll. When all you have to contribute is a kind word, a listening ear, or a smile...

These everyday and ordinary acts of service, when performed under the extraordinary circumstances of chronic pain, are seen by God as extravagant acts of sacrifice. I am convinced that God looks down on these sacrifices in the same way that he looked at the widow's mite. So many give out of an abundance of health, using up only a small portion of their strength each day, but those in chronic pain give out of a poverty of health, giving away everything we have and all the strength we have to live on.

When we give out of what we have, no matter how small, it is greatly pleasing to the Lord. Jesus looks on these sacrifices and says, "you have done more than all of those who give out of abundance."

Called to Serve

This is what I believe. Our time on earth is short, Scripture calls all Christians to some form of work and service, and we do not get a free pass because we are physically disabled and chronically pained. At times, I can spend so much time feeling sorry for myself that I forget there is work to do. And nothing in the Bible says that chronic pain exempts me from God's work.

God calls us to use what we have been given, no more and no less. In the last chapter, we explored what it means to rest when we have used everything up, and in this chapter we will consider what it means to work when we feel like we have nothing to offer. This is the other side of the coin, for there is an ugly side to rest, a sinful side to rest that turns to wallowing and self-pity. If we aren't careful with rest, treating it with caution and respect, it is possible to sway too far to the other side. For some, the struggle gets turned on its head, as we reject our God-given capabilities and begin to feel only self-pity and self-inflicted misery.

There are times when instead of humbly offering our two cents, we mope to God about how unfair life is and how unfair he was to give us nothing to work with. Instead of looking and finding the gifts and abilities that God has given us, like all people regardless of health status should do, we become so fixated on our inabilities, weaknesses, and limitations that we become frozen, unable to move forward. We forget that as long as we are living, breathing, and conscious, we have *something*, as small as it may be, to offer.

Sometimes we need a cup of cold water thrown in our faces to draw us out of our self-pity and despair. There is work to do. At the end of the day, there isn't time to wallow in what we can't do or pine for who we used to be. We step out of our self-pity by believing that God can use us even though we are in pain, maybe even because of our pain, to do his good work.

We have been given gifts and capabilities that the world can use. We are not the only ones who are hurting, and we are not the only ones who need help. Can we stop feeling sorry for ourselves? Can we move out of self-pity and consider how we might be a part of alleviating the suffering that surrounds us?

Following God's commands to serve doesn't happen by ignoring the reality of our decaying bodies. It is a simple fact that chronic pain leaves us unable to serve in the same manner or capacity as individuals in health. There are times when all Christians are called to serve when it hurts, when it is inconvenient, and when it leads to painful after-effects. But it is also important to wrestle with the extent of pain we are called to endure.

Should we purposefully serve to the point of uncontrollable pain in which the emergency room becomes our only option for pain management? Should we push ourselves to greater and greater levels of disability for the sake of service? I don't believe so. I believe there is a point in which pushing our bodies past the limit is a form of misusing and abusing this temple that God has given us (I Corinthians 6:19-20). And in a practical sense, working to the point of burnout and pain that leaves us bedbound is not helpful to anyone, as we lose our ability to complete tasks that may have been accessible to us before we pushed ourselves over the edge.

This is an issue that requires an attentive wisdom as we follow God's commands and accept his grace in our lives of work. And I am convinced that for those of us who are physically limited, there are ways and manners of serving that honor and obey God's calling on our lives, but also protect from relapse and burnout. It is possible to use what God has given us, and then stop, free from guilt.

Equipped to Serve

We get to participate in both rest and service, and God's promises concerning work free us from obsessing over finding the perfect balance. In the last chapter, we found the basis of our rest in Ephesians 2:8-9 which tells us, "For by grace you have been saved through faith. And this is not your own doing; it is the gift of God, not a result of works, so that no one may boast."

To find the basis of our work, we need only read the next verse. Once we accept the free gift of salvation, we then wrestle with our role as, "God's handiwork, created in Christ Jesus to do good works, which God prepared in advance for us to do" (Ephesians 2:10). Our good works flow out of our salvation and love for God, as we desire to do good things for the God who created and saved us.

Ephesians 2:10 holds life-giving news for those of us who feel incapable because of chronic pain. If we are God's handiwork, it follows that he handcrafted us in specific and thoughtful ways. And if God prepared these good works in advance, I feel quite certain that as he planned them, he took into consideration our personalities, abilities, strengths, weaknesses, and physical capabilities.

We are hand-crafted individuals, perfectly suited for the specific work God prepared for us in advance. I sometimes feel like God is pulling a trick on me, cunningly telling me to work and then making me incapable of following through. But even as I feel this way, I remember this verse and know this is not in his character. Quite the opposite, he is asking us to serve in ways that were carefully planned out in advance for us, chronic pain and all.

I stopped doubting that God had prepared works in advance for me when he started showing up in my life of work in incredible ways. I started studying to become a counselor in 2010, and towards the end of completing my counseling degree, my internship unexpectedly fell through at the last minute. My school gave me a week to find a new one, when the first one had taken me four months to find. At the time it certainly felt hopeless. I knew it was not the end of the world, but it would mean a six-month delay before I could continue my degree. That week I sat reading a counseling book in Starbucks. The woman across from me looked at me reading and asked if I, by any chance, needed a counseling internship. *God, is this actually happening?*

When God showed up in this way, it struck me to my core. It felt as though God was speaking directly to the fears of my heart, providing a gift-wrapped sign that he had not forgotten me. I didn't know where he would take me, but wherever it was, he would make it happen and I could trust him.

That is not the only time God has shown up as I slowly work my way through the process of becoming a licensed counselor. Several years after my internship, I desperately needed a job that would enable me to get client hours towards licensure while also accommodating my limitations due to chronic pain. I wrote out a list of ridiculous necessities in my journal and doubtfully prayed that God would provide. I couldn't work more than four hours in a row or more than 7 hours in a week. I needed days off between each work day, and I needed hours that didn't conflict with my other very part-time job. The list went on and on with various other specifications.

That Saturday I sent out two resumes. I received a phone call two days later that next Monday, interviewed on Wednesday, did a second interview later that afternoon, was offered and accepted the job that same evening. And it had everything that I needed. Every single one of the seemingly impossible requirements that I had laid out and more. *God are you serious?*

My point is this. If God has a work he wants you to do, he will provide a way for it to happen. There is no barrier too great that he can't make it fall with a word, with a providential encounter, with a perfect timed job offer that accommodates your pain.

I don't mean that God guarantees he will provide you with a perfect job or opportunity. I don't mean God promises me that all of my career plans will come to fruition. All I am saying is that whatever God desires from you and from me, he will make attainable. He will equip you and provide for you so you can complete the work he has prepared for you.

God also promises that it is his grace and not our own physical strength that gives us the ability to do his good work. His grace gives us "abundance for every good deed" (II Corinthians 9:8). Somehow, in some way, we are ready and able to complete the service and work God has planned for us. We begin by resting in this, and then we get down to the business of figuring out what work God has prepared for us in our day-to-day lives.

Chapter 3 Journaling Questions

1. Do you tend towards a life of guilt in which your push yourself to do more than your body can physically handle? Give some examples of how this might be the case.

2. Or do you tend towards a life of self-pity, believing you have nothing to offer? Give some examples of how this might be the case.

3. Based on your answers to the last two questions and your assessment of whether you tend towards guilt or self-pity, how should you move forward?

CHAPTER 4

Practical Work and
Service When You Have Chronic Pain

I believe that those of us with chronic pain are more capable than we know, and with God working through us, there are no limits to how he might use us. Not only are we more capable than we know, but I believe that sometimes our physical limitations leave us especially qualified to serve in certain capacities. Chronic pain leads to a dynamic in which we are beset with severe weakness, requiring much from others, but these weaknesses also form the basis of strengths that never would have surfaced without chronic pain.

My own health problems started the same month I began studying to be a counselor. I often look back on this "coincidence" and see the hand of God. More than needing the knowledge that comes from books and papers and learning, to become a person qualified to counsel those in suffering, I needed to know what it felt like to suffer. Yes, I needed someone to teach me the "how's" of counseling, but so much more, I needed chronic pain to teach me the wisdom that could only come through walking my own pilgrimage of pain.

To help others in their suffering, I needed to be personally acquainted with grief, loss, and pain. To counsel well, I needed to know the comfort of Christ through the hardest of times, that I might comfort others with the comfort I had received. To point others towards the God who allows suffering, I needed to learn how to follow after God when nothing made sense. Only when chronic pain taught me to feel pain, endure pain, and run after God in my pain, was I ready to meet others in their pain.

This is my story, and I believe there is a version of this story for you. Take a moment to consider how chronic pain has formed you into the person you are today. I believe it has, in different ways for each of us. Chronic pain, illness, and disability are painful yet effective teachers. They have an intense propensity to mold us and form us in empathy, compassion, and wisdom, enhancing our ability to be the hands and feet of God.

Chronic pain can mold us into prayer warriors, encouragers, and wise listeners. Chronic pain can be the catalyst that creates comforters, counselors, and teachers. Chronic pain changes and forms our character, in some ways enhancing our ability to advance the Kingdom of God.

Creative Service

Perhaps you can agree that chronic pain changes our hearts and our minds, readying us for God's work. But, that does us little good if we are unable to move, sit, and walk. Being spiritually equipped by chronic pain seems like a waste if we are stuck in our homes or unable to leave our beds. Even though I am blessed with the ability to work outside of my home, I still often feel like the few hours of counseling I am able to manage each week are nothing, so small that I wonder if it is even worth it. I once again return to my questions. *God, why would you equip me, but then not give me the physical strength I need to work?*

But I am learning that counseling for a few hours outside my home each week is only one small piece of the ministry God has planned for me. For those of us in chronic pain, our couches can become our desks and our bedrooms can become our offices. Our computers can become our means of reaching the world, and our homes can become a hub of great ministry and service, if we are willing to get a bit creative and go against the conventional grain. We may work slowly; we may only be able to work a few hours each day or each week; but our small acts carried out persistently over time can accumulate into great things.

In my interaction with individuals in the online chronic pain and illness community, I have seen incredible work come out of great suffering and unimaginable limitation.

Ginny is a woman in my online small group who experiences daily severe pain from Ehlers-Danlos Syndrome and various other chronic illnesses. The moment you meet Ginny you can tell that she has is both brilliant and kind. For many years Ginny worked as a licensed attorney, adjunct law instructor, and visiting graduate school professor, while managing a training and consulting practice on the side. Over the years, as her conditions progressed, Ginny had to give up her meaningful places of work, one by one, and she is now no longer able to work as she used to.

Losing a career in this manner is devastating. Ginny and many others like her spend years getting an education and building a career, only for chronic pain and illness to swoop down and make work impossible. It can feel like decades of education and experience are now being put to waste. These feelings are not easy to navigate, but I can personally attest that Ginny's past experiences are far from wasted, as she puts her skills to work in new ways and in new arenas.

Ginny continues to use the same analytical thinking skills, research ability, attention to detail, and inquisitive nature she used to excel as an attorney to make a clear difference in the lives of many individuals with chronic pain and illness. When problems arise for individuals in our small group, Ginny is our problem-solver, researcher, and voice of reason. Somehow she always manages to find the most relevant, applicable, and helpful medical advice for whatever problem might ail us. She constantly uses her connections in various chronic pain and illness communities to bring people and solutions together. It is hard to put into words how meaningful and practical her work has been. I don't know what we would do without her.

My dear friend Christine is a full-time mom and wife who serves and loves her family on top of managing chronic pain conditions that are a full-time job in themselves. I think of all the days when just caring for myself has felt like more than I can handle, and I am in awe of mothers with chronic pain who selflessly care for their children when their own bodies are failing.

Beyond her role as a mother, Christine is proof to me of the powerful ministry of being someone's friend. She is my listening ear, my faithful companion, my wise counsel for problems that arise out of chronic pain. She is the one who walks alongside me from afar, encourages me, laughs with me, and advises me. She makes my days lighter just by being my friend.

Several of my friends with chronic pain have left careers that were physically challenging to pursue other careers that accommodate their pain. My friend Jeni used to work as a respiratory therapist, but had to quit when her job became too physically demanding. She has since started school to become a health coach for individuals with chronic pain. She plans to start a business that she will run online from home through Skype and telephone sessions. Dorothy also worked in the medical field as a nurse until her daily headaches and frequent migraines prevented her from continuing in this line of work. Undefeated, Dorothy has decided to pursue an M.Div., and she plans to use this degree to work in a ministry setting in the future.

Many of my friends who are unable to work outside of the home because of their chronic conditions have found their place of service through writing blogs, books, and poetry. I did not realize the power of words until I desperately needed the wisdom of those who had walked the same paths of suffering before me. Their words make me, and many others, feel less alone. Their words give me wisdom when I don't know how to move forward. Many of these wonderful individuals are missionaries from their homes, speaking gospel hope and truth, providing answers the world cannot give.

I could go on and on and tell you about individuals I know who lead chronic pain support groups, advocate for others with chronic pain and disability, and create informational websites to assist others with similar conditions. I could tell you about Linda who takes care of rescue dogs despite constant daily migraines and Kathy who created a thriving jewelry business that she manages from home.

I could tell you about people who were forced to quit their jobs as nurses, lawyers, teachers, counselors and web designers, and have since started businesses in these same fields from home. I could tell you about those who create incredible art, make and sell practical products, and volunteer for organizations and efforts around the world. And they do it all from home. They do it without ever leaving their beds. They create, sell, encourage, advocate, counsel, write, lead, coach, pray, listen, befriend, administrate, problem-solve, and serve within the physical strengths and limitations God has given them.

They know, as I know, and as you can know, that chronic pain does not derail our ability to have an impact on this world. We just have to get creative. Our hours, days and weeks of forced rest don't need to go to waste. We feel incapable and helpless to do anything, but this is not reality.

Moving Forward

Whatever you love, whatever your passion, whatever your gift, I believe there is a way to use it, even if your pain prevents you from moving, walking, sitting, and concentrating for long periods of time. The following questions can help you consider next steps and actions that God might be inviting you to take. I encourage you to read the remainder of this chapter with a journal and pen in hand, prayerfully seeking God's will for your life.

Consider your gifts, resources, and natural talents.

Chronic pain can complicate the process of knowing, understanding, and using the gifts and resources God has given us. A few years back, I took a personality test that was supposed to reveal my gifts, strengths and personal characteristics. Each question plunged me further and further into an identity crisis, leaving me with tears of anger and confusion.

So many thoughts ran through my mind. *How am I supposed to answer a question about how likely I am to do something that I physically can't do because of the pain? Should I answer the question in light of how I used to be before pain, how I am in the midst of my pain, or how I hope to be if the pain goes away? Which of my actions are controlled by my pain and which are controlled by my personality? WHO AM I?*

Many of the questions on this test assumed that I was able-bodied. I wasn't. The test ignored the sizeable portion of the population who may have a great desire to bring someone a casserole and would do this in a heartbeat if they were able, but physically can't. It ignored that someone may have the gift of service or leadership or evangelism or acts of mercy, but not carry that gift out in an expected or traditional manner.

I believe that our good Father gives us gifts, strengths, and resources that transcend our able-bodied or disabled status. I believe we have a God who gives us gifts that can be used, in some manner, regardless of our physical limitations. The test I took was merely a man-made and flawed depiction of the beautiful picture of service God has authored in Scripture.

There is no escaping the fact that chronic pain limits the ways in which we can use the gifts God has given us. But chronic pain does not take away these inherent gifts, strengths, and resources. As you answer the following questions, don't let thoughts about your limitations get in the way. Just list the ways that God has gifted you, and later we will brainstorm how you might use them.

1. What are your gifts and natural talents?

2. How have you excelled in the past?

3. What physical, emotional, spiritual, financial, and material resources has God given you?

Brainstorm a list of possible ways to work or serve. It's time to brainstorm. The beauty of brainstorming is in the freedom it gives you to write down *anything* that spontaneously comes to mind. It increases creative, out-of-the box thinking, an important skill for those of us with chronic pain. Many of your ideas won't pan out, and that is completely OK. Simply write ideas out as they come to mind, and sift through them later. Brainstorming pushes you to defy limitations, envision beyond practicalities, and come up with ideas that you never would have considered if you were thinking logically. Use some of the following questions to jog your brain:

1. Do you have training that you thought was unusable now that you can no longer work outside of your home? If so, how might you transfer that training into a work-from-home career or avenue of service? Most careers can be creatively adapted to enable you to do them in some capacity from home.

2. If you had the courage to ask for accommodations, what could you do that you can't do now?

3. Is there something you would like to be a part of that you could join through electronic means such as Skype or FaceTime?

4. What could you give up that would give you energy to focus on things that are more important to you and to God? Could you get help in an area so you could focus on other areas of service that are more fitting to your skills? For example, could you have your groceries delivered or have someone clean your house so you can save energy to serve elsewhere?

5. That thing you want to do – could you host it in your home and have people come to you? List some possible ideas.

6. Have you looked into volunteering from home? What might this look like?

7. Have you researched online opportunities in your area of interest, expertise, or training? What do you find as you research?

8. Are you downplaying the impact you could have in an area of service that doesn't seem "big" enough? For example, perhaps praying, listening, and encouraging are your strengths or spiritual gifts, but you don't practice them often because they don't seem like a big deal. Maybe they are. What might some of these areas be?

9. Are pride, shame, or self-pity stopping you from moving forward? If they weren't there, what would you be free to do?

Pick one thing. Go back over your list and pick one thing. Just one. Write it in the space below as a commitment that you will give it a try. Move forward with it and see what God does in your life and the lives of those around you.

A Final Note

As you consider how God might be calling you to serve, perhaps you are feeling overwhelmed. Sometimes I feel exhausted just thinking about the effort it takes to reach out and give when our bodies are flaring and screaming at us to stop. There is hope for this exhaustion. There is hope for those times when we become weary of doing good.

Something wonderful happens when we freely give of ourselves, even out of our own suffering, hurt, and pain. When we give wisely, service ceases to drain us of our energy and begins to fill us up with new life. When we step out and serve, we experience the amazing truth of Proverbs 11:25 that "whoever refreshes others will be refreshed."

It sounds counterintuitive, but I have experienced this truth over and over again. In my own life, there are many areas of service I have cut out to live a life of faithful rest. I am thankful for God's grace, that he allows me to do this without guilt. I can also distinctly remember times when the pain felt so unbearable that I considered quitting life and cutting out *all* of my responsibilities so I could hibernate the months away in my bed.

As I prayed for God's guidance, I realized that God's gift to us when we serve is to lift our spirits and grant us hope for moving forward. Many days I would come home from work feeling physically wrecked and destroyed, but emotionally, mentally, and spiritually renewed. The refreshment I received from a few hours of working was enough to bolster me through the next few days of recovery and increased physical pain.

It truly is more blessed to give than to receive, and I believe with all my heart that serving those around us is one of the most important ways we find healing when the pain does not go away. Serving others draws our attention away from our suffering and towards alleviating the suffering of others. It draws us away from brooding thoughts and feelings of purposelessness, as we grab hold of the work God prepared for us to do.

Serving others has powerful healing capacity, and I have seen it draw many in chronic pain out of dark places of depression, self-pity, and self-loathing. Over and over again, I have seen that helping

38

others has the power to sustain people through the deepest ruins of chronic pain, as we discover we do have something to offer. We do have a reason to get up in the morning. The feelings of purposelessness and lack of meaning that so often surface in the midst of physical limitation are pushed to the side, as we live life the way God intended.

We live life as God intended when we look to Christ for our worth, accept his invitation to rest, and focus on our primary purpose – to glorify God and enjoy him forever. As we worship and glorify our Creator and Sustainer, he points us away from self and towards the weary world that surrounds us, giving us a heart to serve our fellow brothers and sisters. We begin to give of ourselves, not to find our worth, but that God might be glorified through the work that we do. In doing this, we begin to find pieces of healing on this earth, even when the pain doesn't go away.

End Notes

1 Westminster Assembly, Kelly, D. F., Rollinson, P. B., & Marsh, F. T. (1986). The Westminster Shorter catechism in modern English. Phillipsburg, N.J: Presbyterian and Reformed Pub. Co.